SQL and PL/SQL in Practice Series

Volume 3: Ranking and Such for Analytics

Djoni Darmawikarta

Table of Contents

Preface

Ranking and Such for Analytics, the 3rd volume of the *SQL and PL/SQL in Practice* series, is for those who need to learn how to use the Oracle ranking and ranking related analytic functions. The analytic functions make it easier for us to write analytic queries.

The analytic functions cover in this volume cannot have windowing clause. You can learn analytic functions that can have windowing clause from my other book, the 2nd volume of *SQL and PL/SQL in Practice* series: *Windowing for Analytics*.

Book Examples

To learn the most out of this book, try the book examples. Set up your own Oracle database and SQL Developer tool to freely and safely try the examples.

You can download free of charge both the database and the tool from the Oracle website. Appendix A is your guide to install the software; Appendix B shows you how to particularly use SQL Developer to try the book examples.

The examples were tested well on Oracle Database 11g Expression Edition release 2 and SQL Developer version 4.

Note on Examples:

- The book examples are shown as SQL Developer screenshots.
- The number of rows of the table used in the examples is purposely small to facilitate your learning.
- Rows of the table might change from one example to another.

Prerequisite

You must have SQL working skill, particularly writing SQL queries. If you encounter SQL related difficulty in following this book, go to get help to the 1st volume of the book *SQL and PL/SQL in Practice series: Learning the Basics in No Time*.

Chapter 1: RANK

The RANK function returns the rank of a value relative to other values.

- Rank is a positive integer.
- Rows with equal values for the ranking criteria receive the same rank.

In the following query for example we would like to know the rank of $2 price relative to the prices of the other rows of the sales table.

Example 1-1

```
SELECT
  RANK (2) WITHIN GROUP (ORDER BY price)
FROM sales;
```

Rank starts at 1 and increments by 1.

- The rank of the first row (VM with 0.5 price) is 1, 2nd row is 2, 3rd row is 3, and our $2 is hence 4.

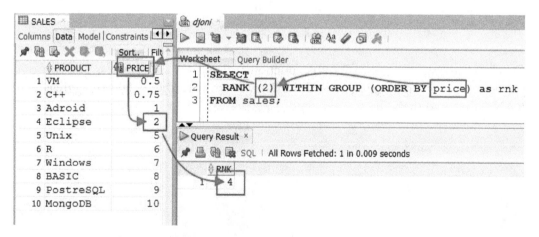

You can also ask the RANK function to find out the rank of a value that does not exist; for example, the rank of $4 price.

Example 1-2

```
SELECT
  RANK (4) WITHIN GROUP (ORDER BY price)
FROM sales;
```

Here's how RANK works:

The function inserts a hypothetical row between the row immediately lower and higher than $4 and evaluates the rank of the hypothetical row, which turns out to be 5.

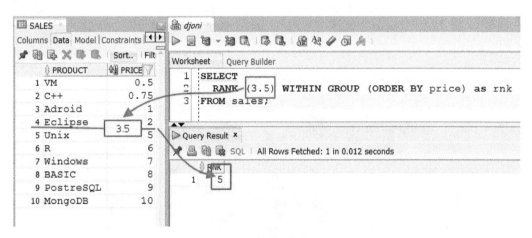

Oracle provides two types of RANK functions: aggregate and analytics. The two previous examples are aggregate RANK. We will cover further details of aggregate RANK first, and then, the analytic type.

Aggregate RANK

Aggregate RANK function has the following syntax.

```
RANK (rank_expression)
WITHIN GROUP (ORDER BY order_by_expression)
```

- A rank_expression, which is the value to be computed for its rank, must evaluate to a constant, which can be numeric, date, and alphanumeric.
- The rank of the rank_expression is evaluated relative to the values of the order_by_expression of the rows returned by the query that uses the function.
- The rank returned by the function is an integer (data type is numeric).

You have seen numeric rank_expression in the previous examples; the next example has date rank_expresssion.

Date rank_expression

The rank_expression in Example 1-3 is a date (September 2, 2016), the rank of which is to be evaluated relative to the order_dt's of the rows of the sales table. The rank of September 2, 2016 turns out to be 6.

Example 1-3

```
SELECT
  RANK (to_date('2016-09-02')) WITHIN GROUP (
ORDER BY
  order_dt) AS rnk
FROM
  sales;
```

Note the use of to_date function to make sure the rank_expression is a date.

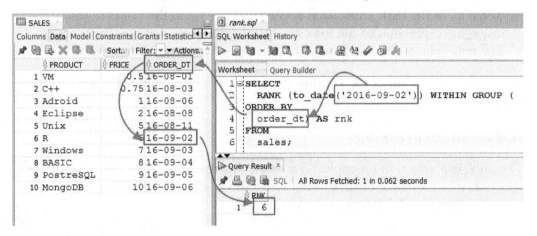

If the rank_expression is not a date, the query will be in error as in the next Example 1-4.

Example 1-4

```
SELECT
  RANK(2) WITHIN GROUP (
ORDER BY
  order_dt ) AS rnk
FROM
  sales;
```

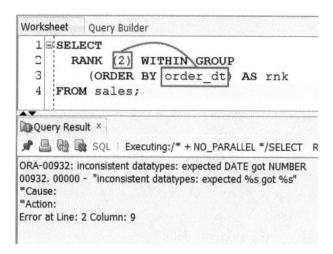

Mandatory ORDER BY

A RANK function requires at least one order_by_expression. The query in Example 1-5 fails, as it does not have any order_by_expression.

Example 1-5, where the rank_expression is alphanumeric, is good.

Example 1-5

```
SELECT
  RANK('R') WITHIN GROUP (
ORDER BY
  (product) ) AS rnk
FROM
  sales;
```

```
Worksheet    Query Builder
  1 ⊟ SELECT
  2      RANK ('R') WITHIN GROUP (ORDER BY (product) ) AS rnk
  3   FROM
  4     Sales;
```

```
▷ Query Result ×
📌 🖨 🔁 📇 SQL   All Rows Fetched: 1 in 0.004 seconds
       RNK
   1      7
```

Example 1-6 fails without the order_by_expression, product.

Example 1-6

```
SELECT
  RANK('R') WITHIN GROUP (
ORDER BY () ) AS rnk
FROM
  sales;
```

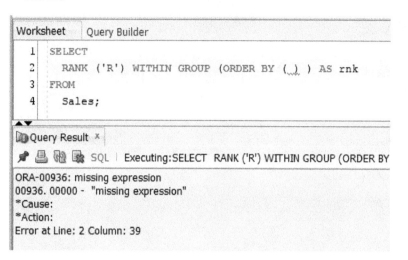

The following also fails without the ORDER BY at all.

Example 1-7

```
SELECT
  RANK('R') WITHIN GROUP () AS rnk
FROM
  sales;
```

Worksheet	Query Builder	
1	SELECT	
2	RANK ('R') WITHIN GROUP () AS rnk	
3	FROM	
4	Sales;	

▲▼

🔲 Query Result ×

📌 🖨 🔐 📇 SQL ┃ Executing:SELECT RANK ('R') WITH

```
ORA-30491: missing ORDER BY clause
30491. 00000 -  "missing ORDER BY clause"
*Cause:
*Action:
Error at Line: 2 Column: 28
```

Query with GROUP BY clause

Recall that the syntax of the RANK function is:

```
RANK (rank_expression)
WITHIN GROUP (ORDER BY order_by_expression)
```

You might have been wondering what the purpose of the WITHIN GROUP is.

It is only effective if the query has a GROUP BY clause. In which case the rank will be by group; each group will rank its rows independent of rows in other groups.

In Example 1-8 the rank of price $2 is evaluated for each of the four product categories.

Example 1-8

```
SELECT category,
  RANK(2) WITHIN GROUP (
ORDER BY
  price ) AS rnk
FROM
  sales
GROUP BY
  category;
```

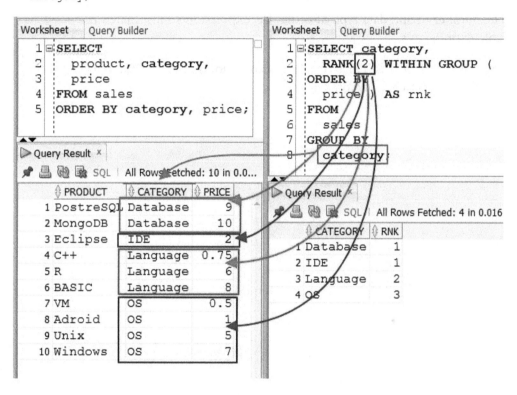

Multiple rank expressions

You can actually have multiple rank_expression's. Here is the RANK syntax with multiple rank_expression's.

```
RANK (rank_expression1 [, rank_expression2]...)
       WITHIN GROUP (ORDER BY order_by_expression1 [,
order_by_expression2] ...)
```

■ The number of and data type of order_by_expression's must match the rank_expression's.

Example 1-9's ORDER BY has two rank_expression's. The first rank_expression is price and the second is sales_dt.

Example 1-9

```
SELECT
  RANK (2, to_date('2016-08-11')) WITHIN GROUP (
ORDER BY
  price, order_dt) AS rnk
FROM
  sales;
```

As there's no row with a price of $2 and order_dt of '2016-08-11', so a hypothetical row inserted after the Eclipse row ($2 and 16-08-08), and its rank is hence 5.

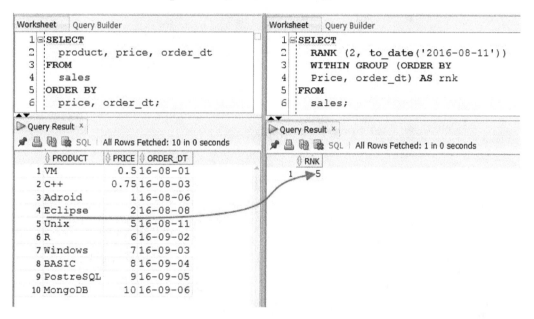

Derived ORDER_BY expressions

The order_by_expression does not need to be just a column.

In Example 1-10, the first order_by expression is quantity * price. The second order_by expression involves CASE logic which produces a value either quantity * 1.5 or 1. The rank_expression (20, 3) evaluates to a rank of 6.

Example 1-10

```
SELECT
  RANK(20, 3) WITHIN GROUP (
ORDER BY
  quantity * price ,
  CASE
    WHEN category = 'Database'
    THEN quantity * 1.5
    ELSE 1
  END) AS rnk
FROM
  sales ;
```

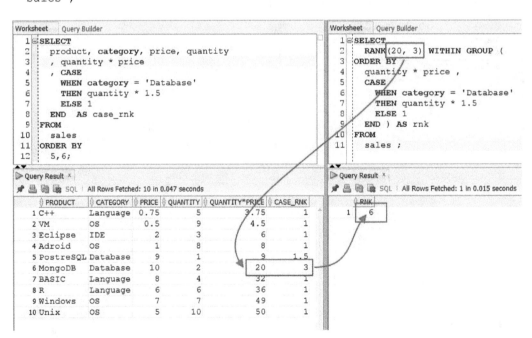

Multiple RANK Function in One Query

A SELECT statement can have more than one RANK function.

Example 1-11 has two RANK functions along with a COUNT function.

Example 1-11

```
SELECT
RANK(3) WITHIN GROUP (
  ORDER BY quantity) rnk_qty,
RANK(3) WITHIN GROUP (
  ORDER BY price) rnk_prc,
  COUNT (*) row_cnt
FROM sales;
```

```
1  SELECT
2     product,
3     quantity, price
4  FROM
5     sales
6  ORDER BY
7     quantity, price;
```

```
1  SELECT
2  RANK(3) WITHIN GROUP (
3    ORDER BY quantity) rnk_qty,
4  RANK(3) WITHIN GROUP (
5    ORDER BY price) rnk_prc,
6    COUNT (*) row_cnt
7  FROM sales;
```

Query Result × All Rows Fetched: 10 in...

	PRODUCT	QUANTITY	PRICE
1	PostreSQL	1	9
2	MongoDB	2	10
3	Eclipse	3	2
4	BASIC	4	8
5	C++	5	0.75
6	R	6	6
7	Windows	7	7
8	Adroid	8	1
9	VM	9	0.5
10	Unix	10	5

Query Result × All Rows Fetched: 1 in 0.015 second

	RNK_QTY	RNK_PRC	ROW_CNT
1	3	5	10

ORDER BY options

Our examples so far apply the default ORDER_BY options.

Here is the syntax of the ORDER_BY.

```
ORDER BY expression [ASC | DESC] [NULLS FIRST | NULLS LAST]
        [, expression [ASC | DESC] [NULLS FIRST | NULLS LAST]
        ...
```

- ASC (ascending) is the default.
- AS NULL is considered the largest, therefore if you specify:
  - ASC and NULLS FIRST, NULL will be the first in the ordered rows.
  - ASC and NULL LAST, NULL will be the last in the ordered rows.
  - DESC and NULLS FIRST, NULL will be the last in the ordered rows.
  - DESC and NULLS LAST, NULL will be the first in the ordered rows.

The query in Example 1-12 has **four** RANK functions.

Example 1-12

```
SELECT
RANK(3) WITHIN GROUP (
  ORDER BY quantity ASC NULLS FIRST) asc_nf,
RANK(3) WITHIN GROUP (
  ORDER BY  quantity DESC NULLS FIRST) desc_nf,
RANK(3) WITHIN GROUP (
  ORDER BY  quantity ASC NULLS LAST) asc_nl,
RANK(3) WITHIN GROUP (
  ORDER BY  quantity DESC NULLS LAST ) desc_nl
FROM sales;
```

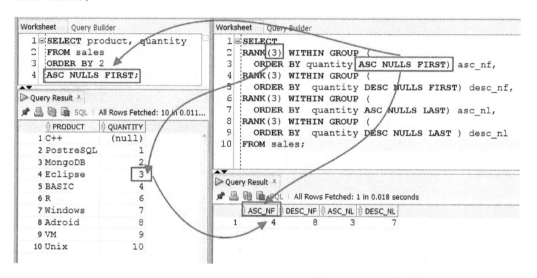

Duplicate Rows

What if we have rows with the same value of rank_expression?

Assume our sales table has two rows with the same price = 2.

In the following query (Example 1-13) both rows with price = 2 are ranked the same = 4.

Example 1-13

```
SELECT
  RANK (2) WITHIN GROUP
      (ORDER BY price) AS rnk
FROM sales;
```

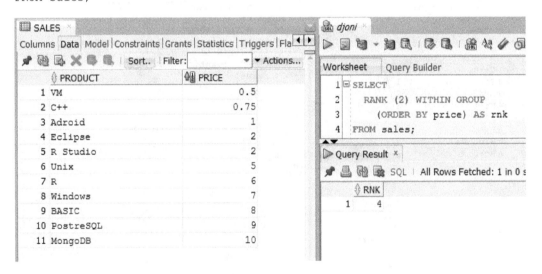

The rank of the next row (Unix) where price = 5 is 6, not 5. The next rank (5) after the duplicate rows is skipped. Two ranks, 4 and 5, have been allocated for the two duplicate rows with the same price = 2, Eclipse and R Studio.

If we have n number of duplicates, n ranks would have been allocated for the n duplicates. Example 1-14 has five duplicates, date = 2-SEP-2016, five ranks have then been allocated for the five duplicates. The rank of the next date (6-SEP-2016) is then 8.

Example 1-14

```
SELECT
  RANK (to_date('06-SEP-16', 'DD-MON-YY')) WITHIN GROUP
      (ORDER BY sales_dt) AS rnk
FROM sales;
```

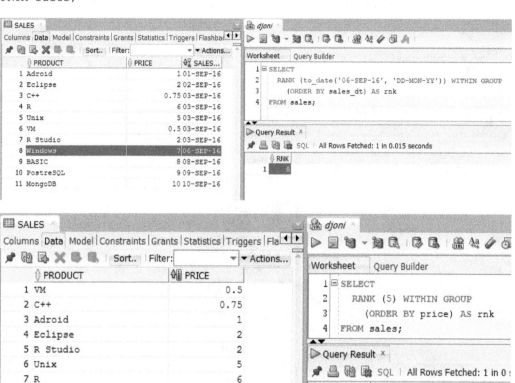

If you want to allocate just one rank for any duplicate rows, use the DENSE_RANK function, which is the subject of Chapter 2.

RANK in ORDER_BY clause

You have seen the use of RANK function in the select list. We can actually also apply the function in the ORDER_BY clause of a query (SELECT statement) as demonstrated in Example 1-15.

Example 1-15

```
SELECT product, category, price
FROM sales
ORDER BY RANK () OVER (ORDER BY price);
```

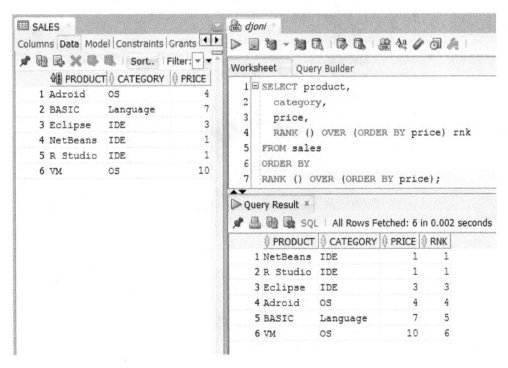

Ordering output rows

The RANK's ORDER BY does not guarantee the order of output rows. You control the order of output row by explicitly specifies with an ORDER BY clause of the query, at the end of the SELECT statement.

Example 1-16

```
SELECT category,
RANK(3) WITHIN GROUP (
  ORDER BY quantity) rnk_qty,
RANK(3) WITHIN GROUP (
  ORDER BY price) rnk_prc,
  COUNT (*) row_cnt
FROM sales
GROUP BY category
ORDER BY 1, 2, 3;
```

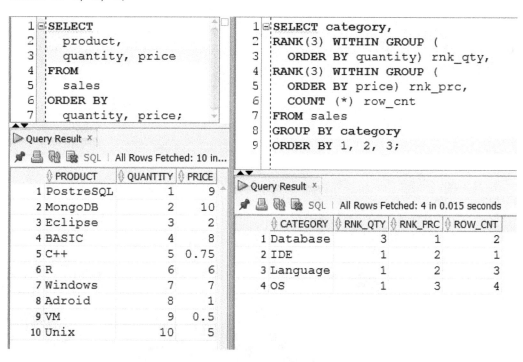

Analytic RANK

Syntax is of the analytic type is as follows.

```
RANK ( ) OVER ([query_partition_clause] order_by_clause)
```

- The query_partition_clause is optional.
- The order_by_clause specifies the order of the rows to be ranked.

Let's compare the aggregate type to the analytic type.

The first difference is that while the aggregate rank returns one row and one column, the analytic rank returns all rows with any column you specify. The two queries in Example 1-17 shows the comparison.

Example 1-17

```
-- aggregate
SELECT
  RANK (2) WITHIN GROUP (ORDER BY price)
FROM sales;
-- analytic
SELECT product,
  RANK () OVER
  (ORDER BY price) anly
FROM sales;
```

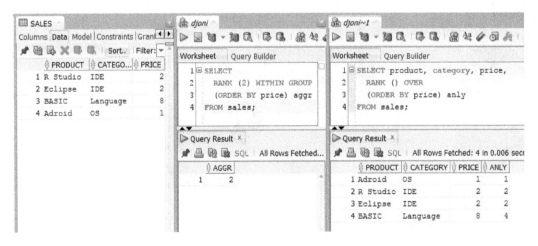

The other difference is the way of grouping. With aggregate rank you apply a GROUP BY clause at the query, not within the RANK function. With analytic rank, you apply a PARTITION_BY clause inside the function. This difference is demonstrated in Example 1-18.

Notice the difference on the output:

- Both types return the rank of each group (category).
- Aggregate returns one row of each group, while analytic returns all rows where rows of the same group ranks the same (the IDE rows)

Example 1-18

```
SELECT
  RANK (2) WITHIN GROUP
  (ORDER BY price) aggr
FROM sales
GROUP BY category;

SELECT product, category, price,
  RANK () OVER
  (PARTITION BY category
  ORDER BY price) anly
FROM sales;
```

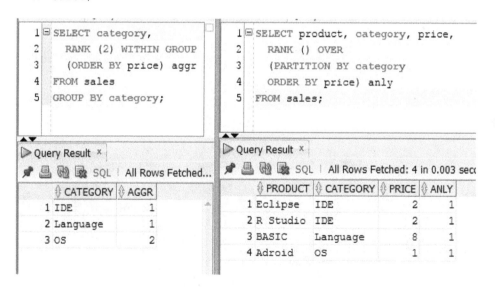

Chapter 2: DENSE_RANK

The difference between RANK and DENSE_RANK is that DENSE_RANK leaves no gaps in ranking sequence when there are ties. That is, if you were ranking a competition using DENSE_RANK and had three people tie for second place, you would say that all three were in second place and that the next person came in third. The RANK function would also give three people in second place, but the next person would be in fifth place.

Similar to RANK, DENSE_RANK also comes in two types: aggregate and analytic.

Aggregate type

The syntax of the aggregate type is as follows.

```
DENSE_RANK(expr [, expr ]...) WITHIN GROUP
  (ORDER BY expr [ DESC | ASC ]
               [ NULLS { FIRST | LAST } ]
         [,expr [ DESC | ASC ]
               [ NULLS { FIRST | LAST } ]
         ]...
  )
```

Here is an example with both RANK and DENSE_RANK in one query so you can easily compare the returns of both side by side.

- While RANK counts a rank for every one of the ordered rows, DENSE_RANK considers tie rows as one rank.

Example 2-1

```
SELECT RANK(5) WITHIN GROUP (
ORDER BY quantity) r,
  DENSE_RANK(5) WITHIN GROUP (
ORDER BY quantity) dr
FROM sales;
```

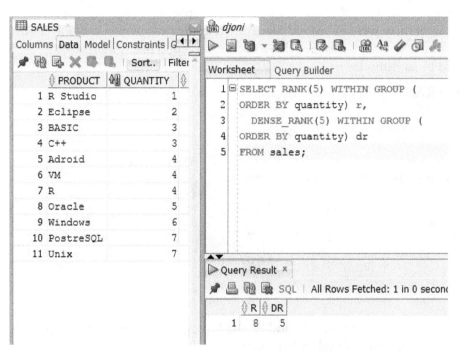

Analytic type

Here is the syntax of the analytic type.

```
DENSE_RANK ( ) OVER ([query_partition_clause] order_by_clause)
```

Here is an example with both RANK and DENSE_RANK in one query so you can easily compare the returns of both side by side.

- RANK counts a rank for every one of the ordered rows, hence the rank of the next row after tie rows jumps.
- DENSE_RANK considers tie rows as one rank, so no rank is skipped.

29

Example 2-2

```
SELECT product, quantity,
RANK()
  OVER (ORDER BY quantity) r,
DENSE_RANK()
OVER (ORDER BY quantity) dr
FROM sales;
```

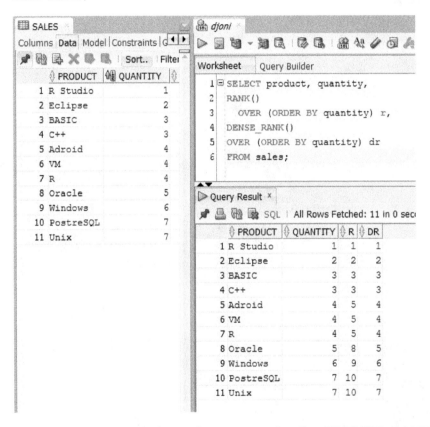

All other options (ordering and treatment of null) of DENSE_RANK function similarly to those of RANK. I do not repeat their coverages in here.

Chapter 3: FIRST/LAST

The FIRST and LAST aggregate functions allow you to rank rows and apply an aggregate function to the top or bottom ranked rows. The aggregation can be on a different column than the column used for ranking.

FIRST

The FIRST function has the following syntax.

```
aggregate_function KEEP ( DENSE_RANK FIRST ORDER BY
  order_by_expression [DESC | ASC] [NULLS {FIRST | LAST}]
  [, order_by_expression [DESC | ASC] [NULLS {FIRST | LAST}]]...)
[OVER query_partitioning_clause]
```

- The aggregate function can be: MIN, MAX, AVG, COUNT, VARIANCE, or STDDEV. Our examples show the uses of the first four.
- The output of the function is the same for all rows in a category. In Example 3-1 below, for examples, the function output min_first for all rows of Database category are 10 and all rows of OS category are 0.5.

The LAST function has a similar syntax, the only difference from that of the FIRST function, is the LAST keyword in place of the FIRST.

```
aggregate_function KEEP ( DENSE_RANK LAST ORDER BY
  order_by_expression [DESC | ASC] [NULLS {FIRST | LAST}]
  [, order_by_expression [DESC | ASC] [NULLS {FIRST | LAST}]]...)
[OVER query_partitioning_clause]
```

Example 3-1 uses two FIRST functions.

- The ranking is on quantities ascending by category.
- The first applies a MIN function on the top ranked rows, the second a MAX function.
- Their outputs are named min_first and max_first.

Example 3-1

```
SELECT product,
  category,
  quantity,
  price,
  MIN(price) KEEP (DENSE_RANK FIRST
ORDER BY (quantity)) over (partition BY category) AS min_fist ,
  MAX(price) KEEP (DENSE_RANK FIRST
ORDER BY (quantity)) over (partition BY category) AS max_first
FROM
  (SELECT *
  FROM sales
  ORDER BY TO_CHAR(sales_dt,'YYYYMMDD')
  ) sales
ORDER BY category,
  quantity,
  product;
```

In the case of Database category, the FIRST ranked row is the MongoDB with quantity = 1 and price = 10, hence the MIN and MAX produce min_first = 10 and max_first = 10 as well.

Query Result ×

SQL | All Rows Fetched: 11 in 0.002 seconds

	PRODUCT	CATEGORY	QUANTITY	PRICE	MIN_FIRST	MAX_FIRST
1	MongoDB	Database	1	10	10	10
2	PostreSQL	Database	2	9	10	10
3	R Studio	IDE	1	2	2	2
4	Eclipse	IDE	2	2	2	2
5	BASIC	Language	3	8	0.75	8
6	C++	Language	3	0.75	0.75	8
7	R	Language	4	6	0.75	8
8	Adroid	OS	4	1	0.5	1
9	VM	OS	4	0.5	0.5	1
10	Windows	OS	6	7	0.5	1
11	Unix	OS	7	5	0.5	1

In the case of Language category, we have **two** FIRST rows (their quantities are the same = 3), hence the MIN produces (picks the minimum price of the two) min_first = 0.75 and the MAX produces (picks the maximum price of the two) max_first = 8.

	PRODUCT	CATEGORY	QUANTITY	PRICE	MIN_FIRST	MAX_FIRST
1	MongoDB	Database	1	10	10	10
2	PostreSQL	Database	2	9	10	10
3	R Studio	IDE	1	2	2	2
4	Eclipse	IDE	2	2	2	2
5	BASIC	Language	3	8	0.75	8
6	C++	Language	3	0.75	0.75	8
7	R	Language	4	6	0.75	8
8	Adroid	OS	4	1	0.5	1
9	VM	OS	4	0.5	0.5	1
10	Windows	OS	6	7	0.5	1
11	Unix	OS	7	5	0.5	1

Query Result ×

SQL All Rows Fetched: 11 in 0.002 seconds

DESC order

Example 3-2 shows the impact of changing the order direction to descending.

- There is no tie ranked rows.

Example 3-2

```
SELECT product, category, quantity, price,
MIN (price) KEEP (DENSE_RANK FIRST
  ORDER BY quantity DESC) over (partition BY category)
      AS min_fs_desc,
MAX (price) KEEP (DENSE_RANK FIRST
  ORDER BY quantity DESC) over (partition BY category)
      AS max_fs_desc
FROM sales
 ORDER BY category, quantity DESC, product;
```

```
1  SELECT product, category, quantity, price,
2  MIN(price) KEEP (DENSE_RANK FIRST
3    ORDER BY quantity DESC) over (partition BY category)
4    AS min_fs_desc,
5  MAX(price) KEEP (DENSE_RANK FIRST
6    ORDER BY quantity DESC) over (partition BY category)
7    AS max_fs_desc
8  FROM
9    sales ;
```

Query Result ×

SQL | All Rows Fetched: 11 in 0.003 seconds

	PRODUCT	CATEGORY	QUANTITY	PRICE	MIN_FS_DESC	MAX_FS_DESC
1	MongoDB	Database	1	10	9	9
2	PostreSQL	Database	2	9	9	9
3	R Studio	IDE	1	2	2	2
4	Eclipse	IDE	2	2	2	2
5	C++	Language	3	0.75	6	6
6	R	Language	4	6	6	6
7	BASIC	Language	3	8	6	6
8	VM	OS	4	0.5	5	5
9	Adroid	OS	4	1	5	5
10	Windows	OS	6	7	5	5
11	Unix	OS	7	5	5	5

LAST

Example 3-2 shows the use of two LAST functions, both with DESC on their ORDER BY.

- Notice the tie LAST rows of the Language and OS categories. The MIN and MAX have to choose (pick) the min and max price, respectively.

Example 3-2

```
SELECT product, category, quantity, price,
MIN(price) KEEP (DENSE_RANK LAST
  ORDER BY quantity DESC) over (partition BY category)
  AS min_fs_desc,
MAX(price) KEEP (DENSE_RANK LAST
  ORDER BY quantity DESC) over (partition BY category)
  AS max_fs_desc
FROM
 sales
 ORDER BY category,
  quantity DESC,
  product;
```

```
1  SELECT product, category, quantity, price,
2    MIN(price) KEEP (DENSE_RANK LAST
3      ORDER BY quantity DESC) over (partition BY category)
4      AS min_fs_desc,
5    MAX(price) KEEP (DENSE_RANK LAST
6      ORDER BY quantity DESC) over (partition BY category)
7      AS max_fs_desc
8    FROM
9     sales
10    ORDER BY category,
11      quantity DESC,
12      product;
```

Query Result ×

SQL | All Rows Fetched: 11 in 0.003 seconds

	PRODUCT	CATEGORY	QUANTITY	PRICE	MIN_FS_DESC	MAX_FS_DESC
1	PostreSQL	Database	2	9	10	10
2	MongoDB	Database	1	10	10	10
3	Eclipse	IDE	2	2	2	2
4	R Studio	IDE	1	2	2	2
5	R	Language	4	6	0.75	8
6	BASIC	Language	3	8	0.75	8
7	C++	Language	3	0.75	0.75	8
8	Unix	OS	7	5	0.5	1
9	Windows	OS	6	7	0.5	1
10	Adroid	OS	4	1	0.5	1
11	VM	OS	4	0.5	0.5	1

Chapter 4: LAG/LEAD

The LEAD/LAG function provides access to a row at a given offset after/prior to the current position.

These functions have the following syntax:

```
{LAG | LEAD} (value_expr [, offset] [, default_value]) [RESPECT
    NULLS|IGNORE NULLS]
  OVER ([partition_clause] order_by_clause)
```

- *Offset* is an optional parameter and defaults to 1.
- *Default_value* is optional and is a **numeric** value returned if offset falls outside of the rows.
- When *IGNORE NULLS* is specified, the value returned will be from a row at a specified lag or lead offset after ignoring rows with NULL. IGNORE NULLS is the default.

Example 4-1 uses LEAD and LAG. Both function's offset is 2. They don't have default_value and query_partition_clause. The rows are ordered by sales_dt.

- For LEAD, the lead value of a row (lead is the output column returns by the function) is the quantity of its next second row.
  - For Android (1st row), for example, its lead is the quantity of C++, which is 3.
  - Another example, for VM row, its lead is the Windows's quantity = 6.
  - For PostreSQL and MongoDB, their leads are null as they don't have any next second row.
- LAG works similarly, but instead of next second row, it takes the quantity of prior second row.
  - For R row, for example, its lag is the quantity of Eclipse, which is 2.
  - The last two rows don't have any prior second row, hence their lag are null.

Example 4-1

```
SELECT product,
  quantity,
  sales_dt,
  LEAD(quantity, 2) OVER (ORDER BY sales_dt) AS "lead" ,
  LAG(quantity, 2) OVER (ORDER BY sales_dt)  AS "lag"
FROM sales;
```

```
1 ⊟ SELECT product,
2     quantity,
3     sales_dt,
4     LEAD(quantity, 2) OVER (ORDER BY sales_dt) AS "lead" ,
5     LAG(quantity, 2) OVER (ORDER BY sales_dt)  AS "lag"
6   FROM sales;
```

▶ Query Result ×

📌 🖨 🔟 📇 SQL | All Rows Fetched: 11 in 0.015 seconds

	PRODUCT	QUANTITY	SALES_DT	lead	lag
1	Adroid	4	01-SEP-16	3	(null)
2	Eclipse	2	02-SEP-16	4	(null)
3	C++	3	03-SEP-16	7	4
4	R	4	03-SEP-16	4	2
5	Unix	7	03-SEP-16	1	3
6	VM	4	03-SEP-16	6	4
7	R Studio	1	03-SEP-16	3	7
8	Windows	6	06-SEP-16	2	4
9	BASIC	3	08-SEP-16	1	1
10	PostreSQL	2	09-SEP-16	(null)	6
11	MongoDB	1	10-SEP-16	(null)	3

Default_value

If you want a value instead of null for the lead/lag of the first/last rows, put in a default value (must be numeric) as demonstrated in Example 4-2 where the default value is 0.

Example 4-2

```
SELECT product,
  quantity,
  sales_dt,
  LEAD(quantity, 2, 0) OVER (ORDER BY sales_dt) AS "lead" ,
  LAG(quantity, 2, 0) OVER (ORDER BY sales_dt)  AS "lag"
FROM sales;
```

```
1 ⊟ SELECT product,
2     quantity,
3     sales_dt,
4     LEAD(quantity, 2, 0) OVER (ORDER BY sales_dt) AS "lead" ,
5     LAG(quantity, 2, 0) OVER (ORDER BY sales_dt)  AS "lag"
6   FROM sales;
```

▶ Query Result ×

📌 🖨 🔢 📇 SQL │ All Rows Fetched: 11 in 0 seconds

	PRODUCT	QUANTITY	SALES_DT	lead	lag
1	Adroid	4	01-SEP-16	3	0
2	Eclipse	2	02-SEP-16	4	0
3	C++	3	03-SEP-16	7	4
4	R	4	03-SEP-16	4	2
5	Unix	7	03-SEP-16	1	3
6	VM	4	03-SEP-16	6	4
7	R Studio	1	03-SEP-16	3	7
8	Windows	6	06-SEP-16	2	4
9	BASIC	3	08-SEP-16	1	1
10	PostreSQL	2	09-SEP-16	0	6
11	MongoDB	1	10-SEP-16	0	3

Respect/Ignore null

If your rows have nulls, you can respect or ignore them, as demonstrated in Example 4-3.

- When you respect null (which is the default), null value (quantity) is considered in the counting of the offset. For example, the Windows row gets null and the Basic row gets 1.
- When you ignore nulls, the null rows are skipped, not considered in the counting of the offset. Hence the Window row gets 1 and the BASIC row gets the default value 0.

Example 4-3

```
SELECT product,
  quantity,
  sales_dt,
  LEAD(quantity, 2, 0) OVER (ORDER BY sales_dt) AS "default/respect",
  LEAD(quantity, 2, 0) IGNORE NULLS OVER (ORDER BY sales_dt) AS "ignore"
FROM sales;
```

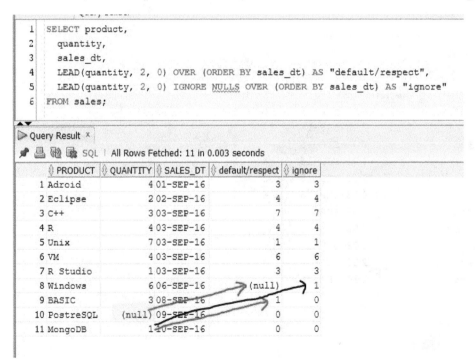

Order_by_clause

As rows are ordered before the determination of the lead and lag, the ORDER_BY clause is significant. The following example compares the outputs of ascending (the default) on the left side to descending on the right side.

Example 4-4

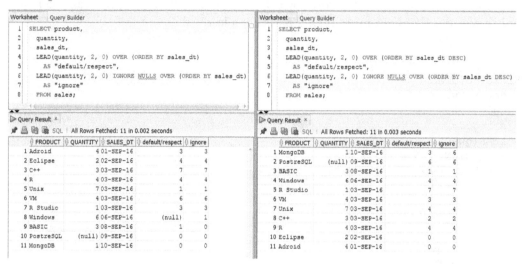

Partition_clause

The partition_clause sets the boundary of rows to be taken into account in determining the lead/lag values.

- Without the partition_clause the boundary is the first and last rows of all rows.

Example 4-5 has partitions the rows by category. As the offset is 2, you can see that only categories that have more than 2 rows get a lead value, not null.

Example 4-5

```sql
SELECT product,
  quantity,
  sales_dt,
  category,
  LEAD(quantity, 2) OVER (
  PARTITION BY category
  ORDER BY sales_dt DESC) "lead partitioned"
FROM sales;
```

	PRODUCT	QUANTITY	SALES_DT	CATEGORY	lead partitioned
1	MongoDB	1	10-SEP-16	Database	(null)
2	PostreSQL	(null)	09-SEP-16	Database	(null)
3	R Studio	1	03-SEP-16	IDE	(null)
4	Eclipse	2	02-SEP-16	IDE	(null)
5	BASIC	3	08-SEP-16	Language	4
6	C++	3	03-SEP-16	Language	(null)
7	R	4	03-SEP-16	Language	(null)
8	Windows	6	06-SEP-16	OS	7
9	VM	4	03-SEP-16	OS	4
10	Unix	7	03-SEP-16	OS	(null)
11	Adroid	4	01-SEP-16	OS	(null)

Chapter 5: CUME_DIST

CUME_DIST calculates the cumulative distribution of a value in a group of values.

- The range of values returned by CUME_DIST is >0 to <=1.
- Tie values always evaluate to the same cumulative distribution value.

Oracle provides types of CUME_DIST: aggregate and analytic.

Aggregate type

Here is the syntax of the aggregate type.

```
CUME_DIST (value_expression) WITHIN GROUP
  (ORDER BY order_by_expression)
```

Here is how the CUME_DIST function works.

- A hypothetical row is inserted. Its position is the value_expression relative among the ordered rows.
- The cumulative distribution of the hypothetical row is calculated, which is the return value of the function.

Let's take a look at Example 5-1 to understand how a cumulative distribution is calculated.

- A hypothetical row with quantity = 1 is inserted.
- The position of the hypothetical row is between row with quality = 1 and the next row that has quality > 1, which is the row with quality = 2. The position is the 2nd row.
- We now have five rows.
- The cumulative distribution of the hypothetical row (the 2nd row) is 2 / 5 = 0.4

Example 5-1

```
SELECT
CUME_DIST(1) WITHIN GROUP
  (ORDER BY quantity) cd1
FROM sales ;
```

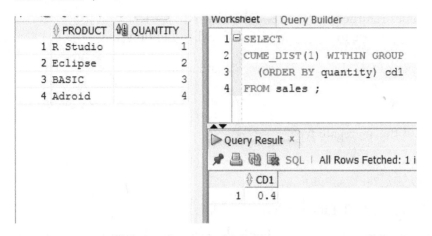

Here is another example.

- In Example 5-2, the query uses five CUME_DIST functions with different value_expression.
- For each of the five functions, a hypothetical row is inserted, the position of which is based on its value_expression.
- For every hypothetical row, its cumulative distribution is calculated based on a total row number of 5.
- Here are examples of the calculation.
  - For CUME_DIST(0), for example, its hypothetical row is the first row, it is inserted before row with quantity = 1 (the R Studio row); hence is cd0 = 1 / 5 = 0.2
  - CUME_DIST(3.99) has its hypothetical row in the fourth row; hence is "cd 3.99" = 4 / 5 = 0.8
  - CUME_DIST(4) (and similarly for CUME_DIST(5)), its hypothetical row is the fifth row, hence cd4 = 5 / 5 = 1.

Example 5-2

```
SELECT
CUME_DIST(0) WITHIN GROUP
   (ORDER BY quantity) cd0,
CUME_DIST(1) WITHIN GROUP
   (ORDER BY quantity) cd1,
CUME_DIST(3.99) WITHIN GROUP
   (ORDER BY quantity) "cd 3.99",
CUME_DIST(4) WITHIN GROUP
   (ORDER BY quantity) "cd4",
CUME_DIST(5) WITHIN GROUP
   (ORDER BY quantity) "cd5"
FROM sales ;
```

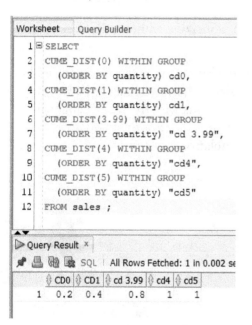

Analytic type

The syntax of the analytic type is:

```
CUME_DIST () OVER ([partition_clause] order_by_clause)
```

- The order_by clause is mandatory
- The partition clause is optional.
- The CUME_DIST computes the relative position of a specified value in a group of values. For a row r, assuming ascending ordering, the CUME_DIST of r is the number of rows with values lower than or equal to the value of r, divided by the number of rows being evaluated (the entire query result set or a partition).

Example 5-3 has two analytic CUME_DIST functions, one without, the other with partition clause.

- Rows with the same price value evaluates to the same cumulative distribution. For example, the three IDE row have the same price = 1, hence all three row evaluates to cd = 0.3 and cdp = 1. The same happens with the three Language rows with price = 6, their cumulative distribution = 0.6. But the two Language rows with price = 8 evaluate to a different cumulative distribution = 1.

Example 5-3

```
SELECT product,
  category,
  price,
  CUME_DIST () OVER ( ORDER BY price) cd,
  CUME_DIST () OVER ( PARTITION BY category ORDER BY price) cdp
FROM sales
;
```

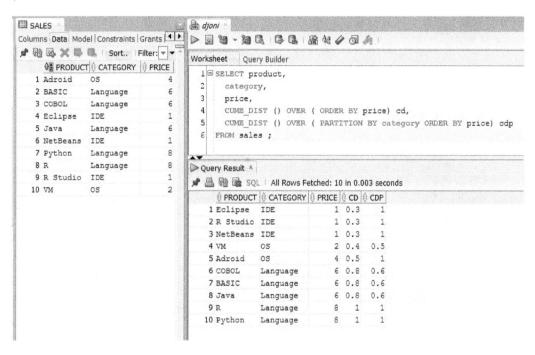

Chapter 6: PERCENT_RANK

PERCENT_RANK is similar to CUME_DIST, but instead of position, PERCENT_RANK uses rank to calculate the percent rank of a value relative to a group of values.

- The PERCENT_RANK of a row is calculated as (rank_of_row − 1) / number_of_row.
- PERCENT_RANK returns values in the range zero to one.
- PERCENT_RANK has two types: Aggregate and Analytic.

Aggregate type

The syntax is of the aggregate type is:

```
PERCENT_RANK (rank_expression) WITHIN GROUP
   (ORDER BY order_by_expression)
```

Here is how the PERCENT_RANK function works.

- A hypothetical row is inserted. Its position is the rank_expression relative among the ordered rows.
- The PERCENT_RANK of a row is calculated as (rank_of_row − 1) / number_of_row

Example 6-1 uses three PERCENT_RANK functions. Notice that we have three rows that have the same quantity = 5. The rank of these three rows are the same = 4. As they are ranked, not dense ranked, Android row with quantity = 7 is ranked 7.

Example 6-1

```
SELECT
  PERCENT_RANK(1) WITHIN GROUP (
ORDER BY quantity) pr1,
  PERCENT_RANK(2) WITHIN GROUP (
ORDER BY quantity) pr2 ,
-- rank(5) = 4
  PERCENT_RANK(5) WITHIN GROUP (
ORDER BY quantity) "pr5",
-- rank(7) = 7
PERCENT_RANK(7) WITHIN GROUP (
ORDER BY quantity) "pr7",
  PERCENT_RANK(10) WITHIN GROUP (
ORDER BY quantity) pr10
FROM
  sales ;
```

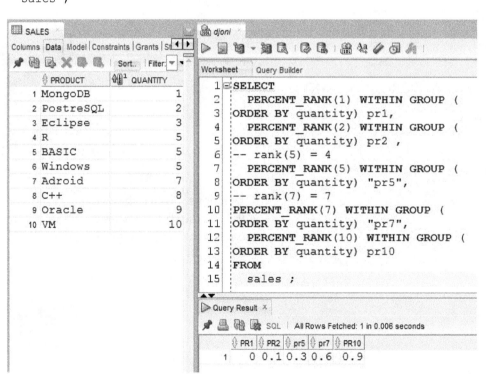

Analytic type

Here is the syntax of the analytic type

```
PERCENT_RANK () OVER ([query_partition_clause] order_by_clause)
```

Example 6-2 has two PERCEN_RANK functions, with and without partition. The query also includes four RANK functions, which aids to show how the two percent ranks are derive.

- The percent rank of a row r is the rank of r minus 1, divided by 1 less than the number of rows being evaluated (all rows or rows in the r's partition).

Example 6-2

```
SELECT product,
  category,
  price,
  rank() over (order by price) r,
  rank() over (order by price) - 1 "r-1",
  PERCENT_RANK () OVER ( ORDER BY price) pr,
  rank() over (partition by category order by price) rp,
  rank() over (partition by category order by price) - 1 "rp-1",
  PERCENT_RANK () OVER ( PARTITION BY category ORDER BY price) prp
FROM sales ;
```

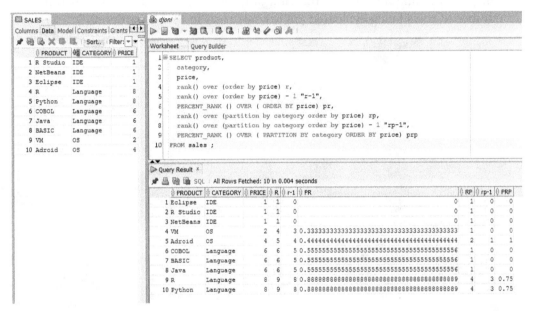

Chapter 7: NTILE

NTILE function divides rows into a specified number of groups called buckets and assigns a bucket number to each row in the partition.

- The bucket number starts at 1 and incremented sequentially by 1.
- Each bucket has the same number of rows if the number of rows (rows returned by the query) divide to it evenly (without a remainder)
- If the number of rows does not divide evenly into the number of buckets, then the number of rows assigned for each bucket will differ by one at most. The extra rows will be distributed one for each bucket starting from the lowest bucket number.

The NTILE function has the following syntax:

```
NTILE (number_of_basket) OVER ([query_partition_clause] order_by_clause)
```

In Example 7-1, we would like to put the rows (ordered by sales_dt) into 4 buckets. The buckets will be numbered 1, 2, 3, and 4.

- The 12 rows divide evenly into the 4 buckets. Each and every bucket has 3 rows.

Example 7-1

```
SELECT product,
  sales_dt,
  NTILE (4) OVER (order by sales_dt) "basket"
FROM sales;
```

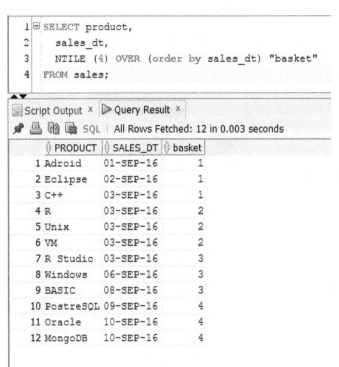

In Example 7-2 the query runs against 11 rows; they don't divide evenly into the 4 buckets.

- As 11 / 4 (number of rows divided by number of buckets) = 2 with a remainder of 3, the first three buckets get an extra 1 row on top of the 2 rows that are distributed to every bucket.

Example 7-2

```
1 SELECT product,
2    sales_dt,
3    NTILE (4) OVER (order by sales_dt) "basket"
4 FROM sales;
```

Script Output × ▷ Query Result ×

📌 🖨 🔁 🔃 SQL | All Rows Fetched: 11 in 0.004 seconds

	PRODUCT	SALES_DT	basket
1	Adroid	01-SEP-16	1
2	Eclipse	02-SEP-16	1
3	C++	03-SEP-16	1
4	R	03-SEP-16	2
5	Unix	03-SEP-16	2
6	VM	03-SEP-16	2
7	R Studio	03-SEP-16	3
8	Windows	06-SEP-16	3
9	BASIC	08-SEP-16	3
10	PostreSQL	09-SEP-16	4
11	Oracle	10-SEP-16	4

If number_of_bucket is not an integer, it will be rounded. In Example 7-3, 5.33 is rounded to 5.

Example 7-3

```
SELECT product,
  sales_dt,
  NTILE ( 5.33) OVER (order by sales_dt) "basket"
FROM sales ;
```

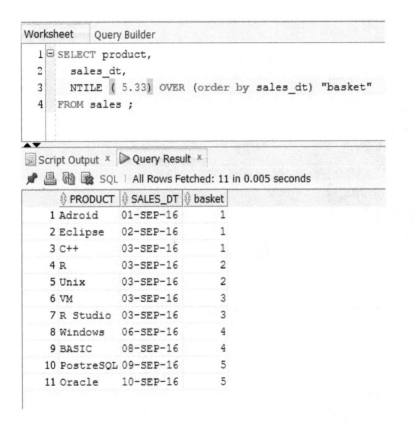

56

Partition-by clause

In Example 7-4 the rows are partitioned by category.

- Each category will have its own buckets.
- Rows from other categories are not considered.

Notice that as the number_of_basket (5) is larger than the number of rows (in every category) the bucket number is as high as the number of rows in the category, there is no bucket number 5.

Example 7-4

```
SELECT product, category,
  sales_dt,
  NTILE (5) OVER (partition by category order by sales_dt) "basket"
FROM sales ;
```

	PRODUCT	CATEGORY	SALES_DT	basket
1	PostreSQL	Database	09-SEP-16	1
2	Oracle	Database	10-SEP-16	2
3	Eclipse	IDE	02-SEP-16	1
4	R Studio	IDE	03-SEP-16	2
5	C++	Language	03-SEP-16	1
6	R	Language	03-SEP-16	2
7	BASIC	Language	08-SEP-16	3
8	Adroid	OS	01-SEP-16	1
9	Unix	OS	03-SEP-16	2
10	VM	OS	03-SEP-16	3
11	Windows	OS	06-SEP-16	4

Chapter 8: ROW_NUMBER

The ROW_NUMBER function assigns a unique number sequentially, starting from 1 as defined by ORDER BY, to each row within the partition. It has the following syntax:

```
ROW_NUMBER ( ) OVER ([query_partition_clause] order_by_clause)
```

- Query_partition_clause is optional.

Example 8-1

```
SELECT
  product,quantity, price ,
  quantity*price,
  ROW_NUMBER ()
  OVER (ORDER BY (quantity*price)) rn
FROM
  sales ;
```

	PRODUCT	QUANTITY	PRICE
1	PostreSQL	1	2
2	MongoDB	2	3
3	Eclipse	3	2
4	BASIC	4	1.5
5	R	5	1
6	C++	5	2
7	Windows	6	1
8	Adroid	7	1
9	VM	8	1.5
10	Unix	9	1

```
1 ≡SELECT
2     product,quantity, price ,
3     quantity*price,
4     ROW_NUMBER ()
5     OVER (ORDER BY (quantity*price)) rn
6 FROM
7     sales ;
```

Query Result ×

SQL | All Rows Fetched: 10 in 0 seconds

	PRODUCT	QUANTITY	PRICE	QUANTITY*PRICE	RN
1	PostreSQL	1	2	2	1
2	R	5	1	5	2
3	BASIC	4	1.5	6	3
4	Eclipse	3	2	6	4
5	MongoDB	2	3	6	5
6	Windows	6	1	6	6
7	Adroid	7	1	7	7
8	Unix	9	1	9	8
9	C++	5	2	10	9
10	VM	8	1.5	12	10

Note that rows 3 to 6 are ties, their quantity * price values (the order_by_expression) are the same, 6.

PRODUCT	QUANTITY	PRICE	QUANTITY*PRICE	RN
1 PostreSQL	1	2	2	1
2 R	5	1	5	2
3 BASIC	4	1.5	6	3
4 Eclipse	3	2	6	4
5 MongoDB	2	3	6	5
6 Windows	6	1	6	6
7 Adroid	7	1	7	7
8 Unix	9	1	9	8
9 C++	5	2	10	9
10 VM	8	1.5	12	10

Query Result ×

SQL | All Rows Fetched: 10 in 0 seconds

ROW_NUMBER is a non-deterministic function

A function is deterministic if, for the same arguments, it always returns the same result.

In Example 8-2 the argument of the RANK function is the ORDER BY **price**. The price column is not unique among the source rows: R Studio and Eclipse have the same price, 2. Note that the source rows are the output of the subquery: (SELECT * FROM sales ORDER BY TO_CHAR (sales_dt, 'YYYYMMDD') ASC)

Example 8-2

```
SELECT product,
  price,
  sales_dt,
  ROW_NUMBER () OVER (ORDER BY (price)) rn
FROM
  (SELECT *
  FROM sales
  ORDER BY TO_CHAR(sales_dt,'YYYYMMDD') ASC
  ) sales ;
```

```
1  SELECT product,
2    price,
3    sales_dt,
4    ROW_NUMBER () OVER (ORDER BY (price)) rn
5  FROM
6    (SELECT *
7    FROM sales
8    ORDER BY TO_CHAR(sales_dt,'YYYYMMDD') ASC
9    ) sales ;
```

Query Result ×

SQL | All Rows Fetched: 11 in 0.004 seconds

	PRODUCT	PRICE	SALES_DT	RN
1	VM	0.5	03-SEP-16	1
2	C++	0.75	03-SEP-16	2
3	Adroid	1	01-SEP-16	3
4	R Studio	2	03-SEP-16	4
5	Eclipse	2	02-SEP-16	5
6	Unix	5	03-SEP-16	6
7	R	6	03-SEP-16	7
8	Windows	7	06-SEP-16	8
9	BASIC	8	08-SEP-16	9
10	PostreSQL	9	09-SEP-16	10
11	MongoDB	10	10-SEP-16	11

The ROW_NUMBER function in the following Example 8-3 has the same argument as in Example 8-2, the ORDER BY price. The source rows (subquery output rows) are now ordered descending. The ROW_NUMBER function does not produce the same output as the previous query.

Example 8-3

```
SELECT product,
  price,
  sales_dt,
  ROW_NUMBER () OVER (ORDER BY (price)) rn
FROM
  (SELECT *
  FROM sales
  ORDER BY TO_CHAR(sales_dt,'YYYYMMDD') DESC
  ) sales ;
```

```
Worksheet    Query Builder
  1 ⊟ SELECT product,
  2      price,
  3      sales_dt,
  4      ROW_NUMBER () OVER (ORDER BY (price)) rn
  5   FROM
  6      (SELECT *
  7      FROM sales
  8      ORDER BY TO_CHAR(sales_dt,'YYYYMMDD') DESC
  9      ) sales ;
```

Query Result ×

SQL | All Rows Fetched: 11 in 0.006 seconds

	PRODUCT	PRICE	SALES_DT	RN
1	VM	0.5	03-SEP-16	1
2	C++	0.75	03-SEP-16	2
3	Adroid	1	01-SEP-16	3
4	Eclipse	2	02-SEP-16	4
5	R Studio	2	03-SEP-16	5
6	Unix	5	03-SEP-16	6
7	R	6	03-SEP-16	7
8	Windows	7	06-SEP-16	8
9	BASIC	8	08-SEP-16	9
10	PostreSQL	9	09-SEP-16	10
11	MongoDB	10	10-SEP-16	11

Example 8-4 and 8-5 add product, which is unique, in the ORDER BY to ensure deterministic row numbers of the tie rows. Now regardless the order of the source rows, the ROW_NUMBER function produces the same result.

Example 8-4

```
SELECT product,
  price,
  sales_dt,
  ROW_NUMBER () OVER (ORDER BY price, product) rn
FROM
  (SELECT *
  FROM sales
  ORDER BY TO_CHAR(sales_dt,'YYYYMMDD') ASC
  ) sales ;
```

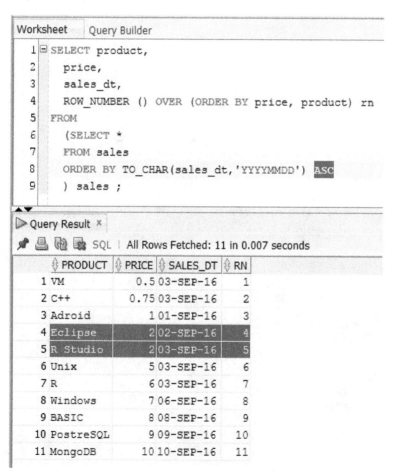

Example 8-5

```
SELECT product,
  price,
  sales_dt,
  ROW_NUMBER () OVER (ORDER BY price, product) rn
FROM
  (SELECT *
  FROM sales
  ORDER BY TO_CHAR(sales_dt,'YYYYMMDD') DESC
  ) sales ;
```

	Worksheet	Query Builder

```
1  SELECT product,
2    price,
3    sales_dt,
4    ROW_NUMBER () OVER (ORDER BY price, product) rn
5  FROM
6    (SELECT *
7    FROM sales
8    ORDER BY TO_CHAR(sales_dt,'YYYYMMDD') DESC
9    ) sales ;
```

▶ Query Result ×

📌 🖨 🐒 📇 SQL | All Rows Fetched: 11 in 0.003 seconds

	PRODUCT	PRICE	SALES_DT	RN
1	VM	0.5	03-SEP-16	1
2	C++	0.75	03-SEP-16	2
3	Adroid	1	01-SEP-16	3
4	Eclipse	2	02-SEP-16	4
5	R Studio	2	03-SEP-16	5
6	Unix	5	03-SEP-16	6
7	R	6	03-SEP-16	7
8	Windows	7	06-SEP-16	8
9	BASIC	8	08-SEP-16	9
10	PostreSQL	9	09-SEP-16	10
11	MongoDB	10	10-SEP-16	11

Chapter 9: RATIO_TO_REPORT

The RATIO_TO_REPORT function computes the ratio of a value to the sum of a set of values.

Its syntax is:

```
RATIO_TO_REPORT (expression) OVER ([partition_clause])
```

- Expression can be any valid expression involving column references or aggregates.
- If the expression value expression evaluates to NULL, RATIO_TO_REPORT also evaluates to NULL, but it is treated as zero for computing the sum of values for the denominator.
- The optional partition_clause defines the groups on which the RATIO_TO_REPORT function is to be computed. If you don't specify the clause, the ratio is computed over the whole query result set.

Example 9-1 does not have any partition clause, so the ratio is computed to the total of prices of all rows. Note that same prices get the same ratio.

Example 9-1

```
SELECT product,
  category,
  price,
  RATIO_TO_REPORT (price) OVER ( ) rtr
FROM sales ;
```

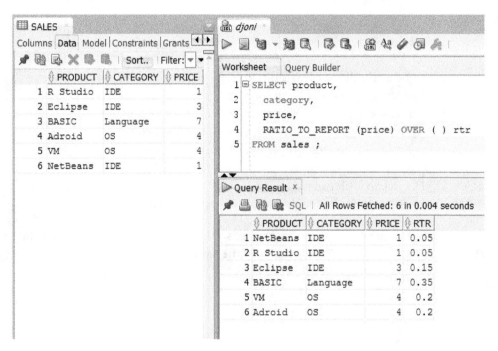

Example 9-2 has a partition clause. The ratio of a row is computed over the rows of its category; in other words, rows of other categories do not get involved in the ratio computation.

Example 9-2

```
SELECT product, category, price,
  RATIO_TO_REPORT (price) OVER
  (PARTITION BY category) rtr
FROM sales;
```

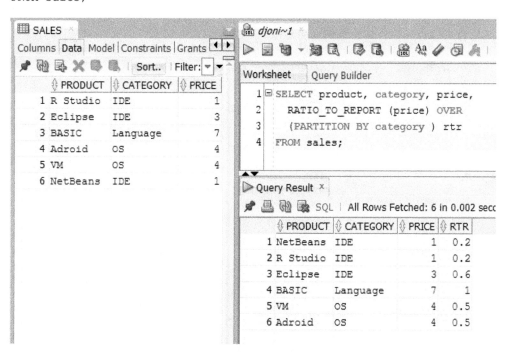

Chapter 10: LISTAGG

The LISTAGG function orders data within each group based on
the ORDER BY clause and then concatenates the values of the list_expression.

Its syntax is as follows.

```
LISTAGG (list_expression [, 'delimiter'])
  WITHIN GROUP (order_by_clause) [OVER query_partition_clause]
```

- The delimiter is a string constant (one or more characters) which separates a value from the next in the output list of the list_expression. If you don't specify it, it defaults to NULL.
- The OVER is optional. If you don't specify, each and every list will have every one of the list_expression.

Example 10-1 uses LISTAGG to list the products delimited by three characters: a space, a pipe |, and a space. The products in a list are ordered by price.

Example 10-1

```
SELECT category, product, price,
LISTAGG (product, ' | ')
  WITHIN GROUP (ORDER BY price)
  OVER (PARTITION BY category) la
FROM sales;
```

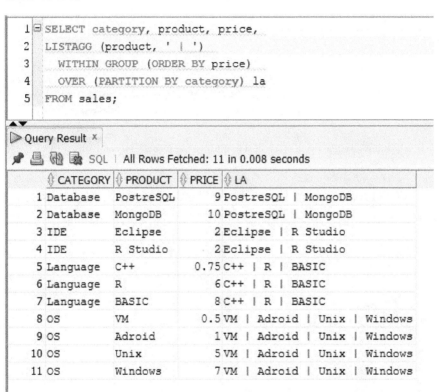

Without OVER clause

If you don't specify the OVER, your query (SELECT statement) needs to have a GROUP BY, as in Example 10-2.

▪ The output is at the GROUP BY level (category), not product row level.

Example 10-2

```
SELECT category,
  LISTAGG (product, ' | ')
    WITHIN GROUP (
    ORDER BY price) la
FROM sales
GROUP BY category;
```

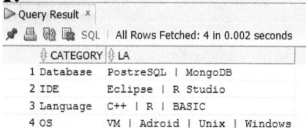

Note

The LISTAGG function is non-deterministic. See Chapter 7: ROW_NUMBER to handle duplicate ordered rows.

Appendix A: Setting Up

This first chapter is a guide to install and set up the Oracle Database 11g Expression Edition release 2 and SQL Developer version 4. Both are available at the Oracle website for download at no charge.

Installing Database Express Edition

Go to http://www.oracle.com/technetwork/indexes/downloads/index.html

Locate and download the Windows version of the Oracle Database Express Edition (XE). You will be requested to accept the license agreement. If you don't have one, create an account; it's free.

Unzip the downloaded file to a folder in your local drive, and then, double-click the setup.exe file.

You will see the Welcome window.

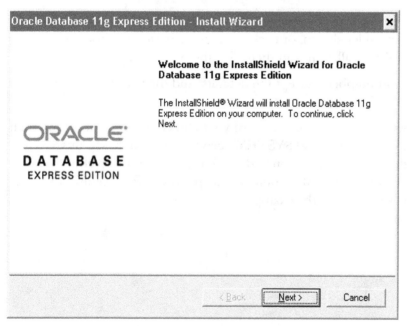

Click the Next> button, accept the agreement on the License Agreement window, and then click the Next> button again.

The next window is the "Choose Destination Location" window.

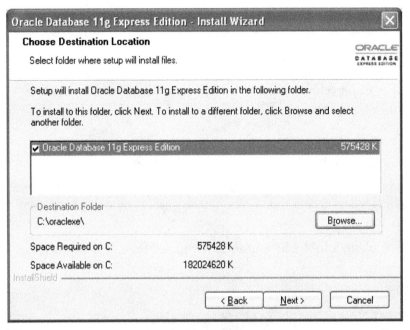

Accept the destination folder shown, or click the Browse button to choose a different folder for your installation, and then click the Next> button.

On the prompt for port numbers, accept the defaults, and then click the Next> button.

On the Passwords window, enter a password of your choice and confirm it, and then click the Next> button. The SYS and SYSTEM accounts created during this installation are for the database operation and administration, respectively. Note the password; you will use the SYSTEM account and its password for creating your own account, which you use for trying the examples.

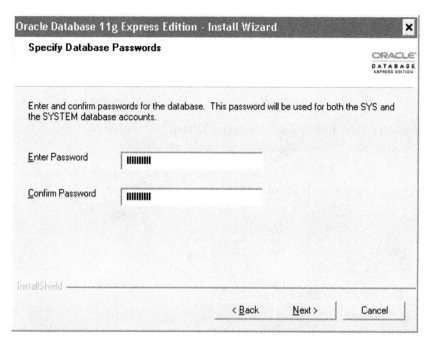

The Summary window will be displayed. Click Install.

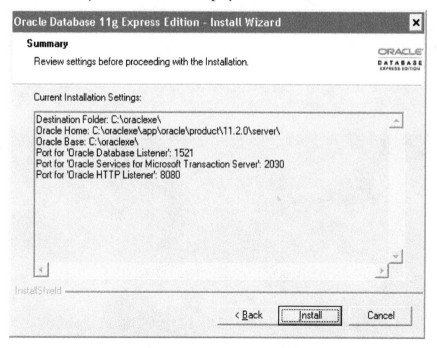

Finally, when the Installation Completion window appears, click the Finish button.

Your Oracle Database XE is now installed.

Installing SQL Developer

Go to http://www.oracle.com/technetwork/indexes/downloads/index.html

Locate and download the SQL Developer. You will be requested to accept the license agreement. If you don't have one, create an account; it's free.

Unzip the downloaded file to a folder of your preference. Note the folder name and its location; you will need to know them to start your SQL Developer.

When the unzipping is completed, look for the sqldeveloper.exe file.

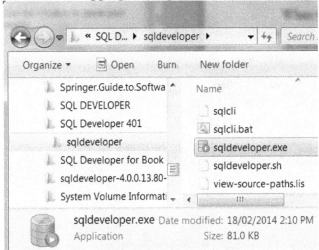

You start SQL Developer by opening (double-clicking) this file.

You might want to create a short-cut on your Desktop.

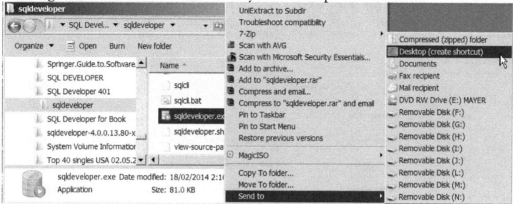

You can then start your SQL Developer by double-clicking the short-cut.

Your initial screen should look like the following. If you don't want to see the Start Page tab the next time you start SQL Developer, un-check the *Show on Startup* box at the bottom left side of the screen.

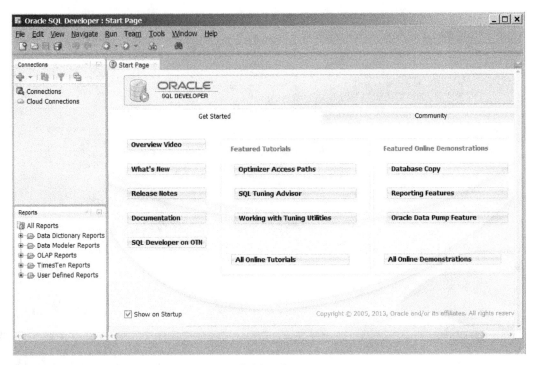

For now, close the Start Page tab by clicking its x.

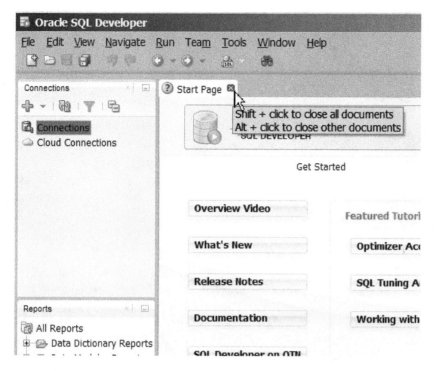

Creating Connection

To work with a database from SQL Developer, you need to have a connection.

A connection is specific to an account. As we will use the SYSTEM account to create your own account, you first have to create a connection for the SYSTEM account.

To create a connection, right-click the Connection folder.

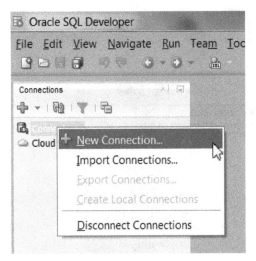

On the New/Select Database Connection window, enter a Connection Name and Username as shown. The Password is the password of SYSTEM account you entered during the Oracle database installation. Check the Save Password box.

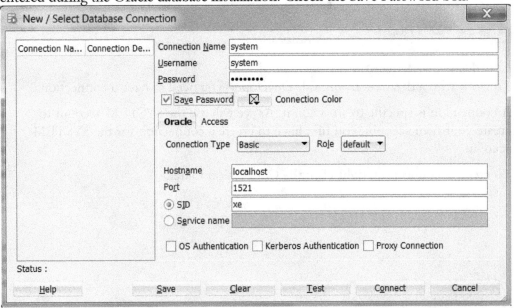

When you click the Connect button, the *system* connection you have just created should be available on the Connection Navigator.

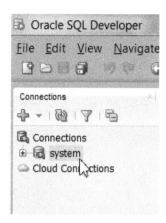

A Worksheet is opened for the system connection. The Worksheet is where you type in source codes.

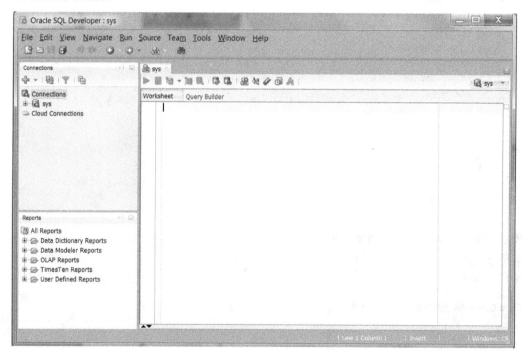

Creating Database Account

You will use your own database account (user) to try the book examples.

To create a new account, expand the system connection and locate the Other Users folder at the bottom of the folder tree.

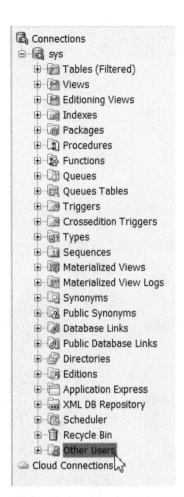

Right click and select Create User.

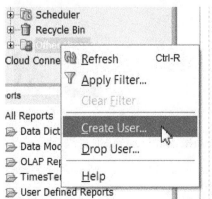

Enter a User Name of your choice, a password and its confirmation, and then click the Apply button. You should get a successful pop-up window; close it.

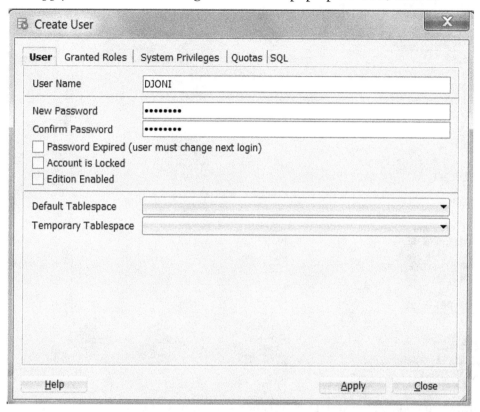

On the Granted Roles tab, click Grant All, Admin All and Default All buttons; then click the Apply button. Close the successful window and the Edit User as well.

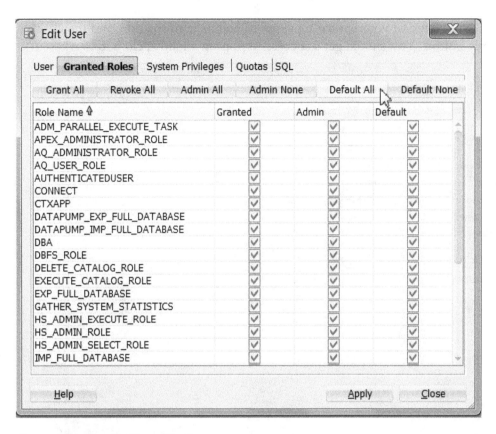

Creating Your Connection

Similar to when you created system connection earlier, now create a connection for your account.

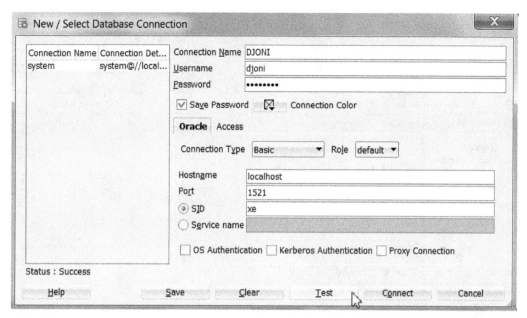

Click the Connect button. A worksheet for your connection is opened (which is *DJONI* in my case).

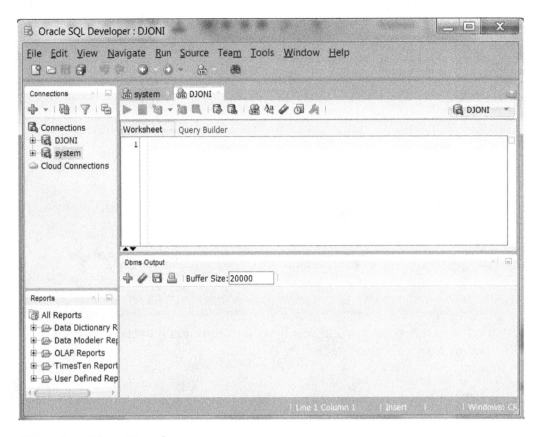

Showing Line Numbers

In describing the book examples I sometimes refer to the line numbers of the program; these are line numbers on the worksheet. To show line numbers, click Preferences from the Tools menu.

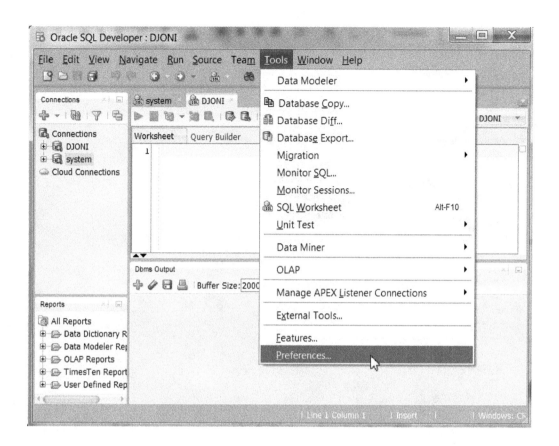

Select Line Gutter, then check the Show Line Numbers. Your Preferences should look like the following. Click the OK button.

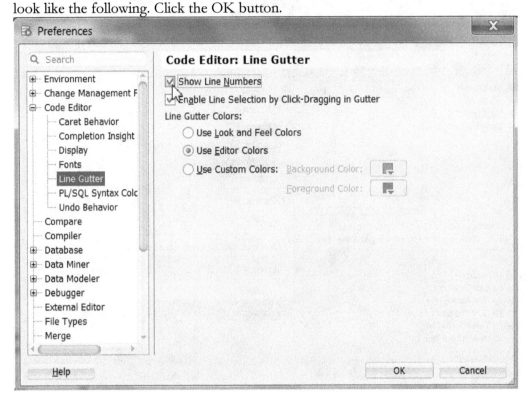

Deleting the *system* Connection

Delete the *system* connection, making sure you don't use this account mistakenly. Click Yes when you are prompted to confirm the deletion. Your SQL Developer is now set.

88

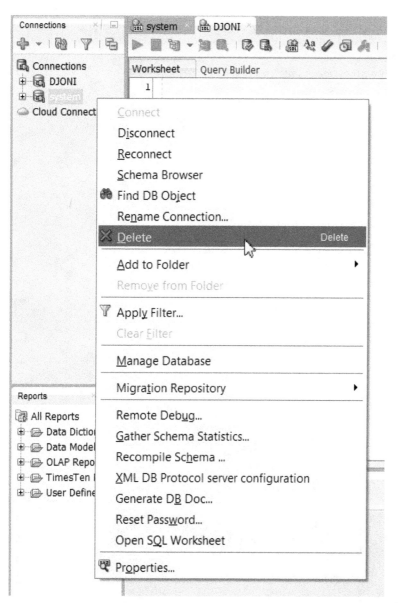

Close the *system* worksheet.

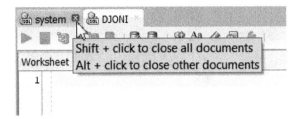

Appendix B: Using SQL Developer

This chapter shows you how to use the SQL Developer features that you will use to try the book examples.

Entering SQL statement

The worksheet is where you enter SQL statement.

Start your SQL Developer if you have not done so. To open a worksheet for your connection, click the + (folder expansion) or double-click the connection name. Alternatively, right-click the connection and click Connect.

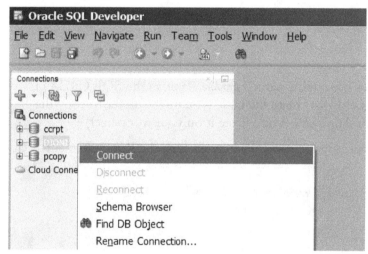

Note the name of the worksheet (tab label) is the name of your connection.

You can type source code on the worksheet.

Appendix A has the source code of all the book examples. Instead of typing, you can copy a source code and paste it on the worksheet.

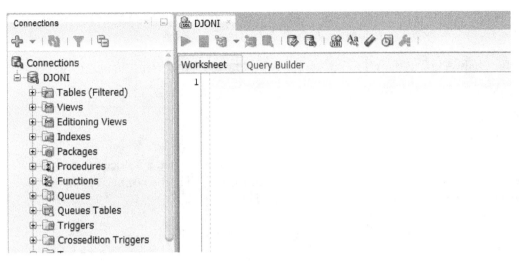

SQL Statement

Some of the book examples use a table named *produce*. Type in the SQL CREATE TABLE statement shown below to create the table (you might prefer to copy the *create_produce.sql* listing from Appendix A and paste it on your worksheet)

You run a SQL statement already in a worksheet by clicking the Run Statement button.

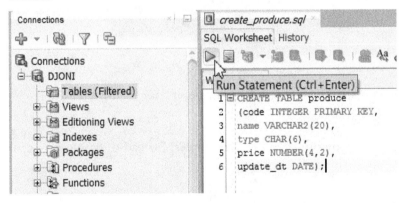

The Script Output pane confirms that the table has been created, and you should see the produce table in the Connection Navigator under your connection folder. If you don't see the newly created table, click Refresh.

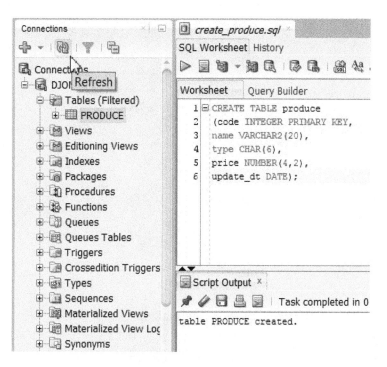

Inserting Rows

As an example of running multiple SQL statements in SQL Developer, the following five statements insert five rows into the produce table. Please type the statements, or copy it from *insert_produce.sql* in Appendix A. You will use these rows when you try the book examples.

Run all statements by clicking the Run Script button, or Ctrl+Enter (press and hold Ctrl button then click Enter button)

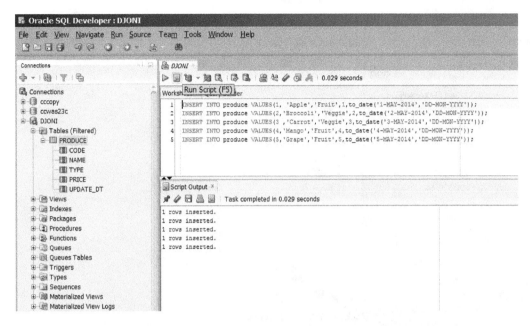

Multiple worksheets for a connection

Sometimes you need to have two or more programs on different worksheets. You can open more than one worksheet for a connection by right-clicking the connection and select Open SQL Worksheet.

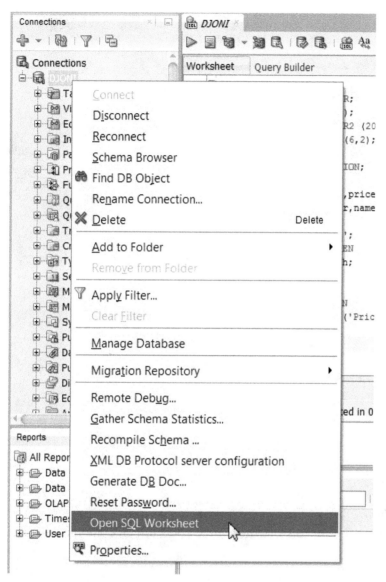

The names of the next tabs for a connection have sequential numbers added.

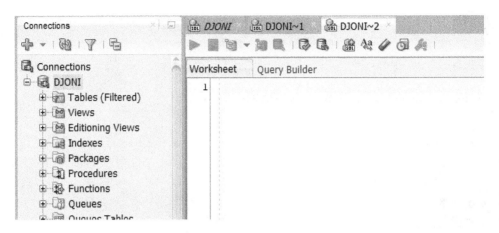

Storing the source code

You can store a source code into a text file for later re-opening by selecting Save from the File menu.

Select the location where you want to store the source code and give the file a name, and then click Save.

Opening a source code

You can open a source code by selecting Open or Reopen from the File menu and then select the file that contains the source code.

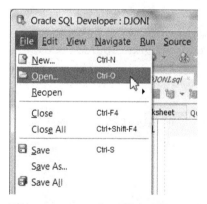

The source code will be opened on a new worksheet. The tab of the worksheet has the name of the file. The following is the worksheet opened for the source code stored as file named running_plsql.sql.

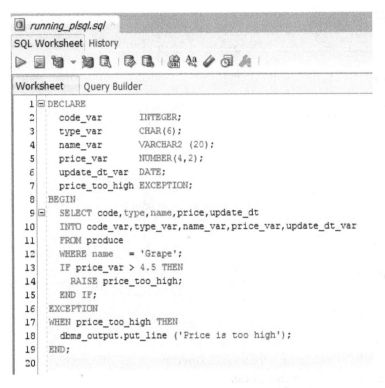

Storing the listings in Appendix A into files

As an alternative to copy and paste, you can store each of the listing into a file and then you can open the file. Note that you must store each program source code into a file.

Running SQL from a file

You can execute a file that contains SQL statement without opening it on the worksheet as shown here.

Clearing a Worksheet
To clear a Worksheet, click its Clear button.

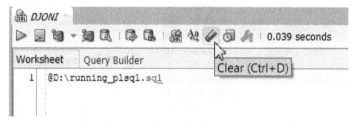

Index

www.ingramcontent.com/pod-product-compliance
Lightning Source LLC
Chambersburg PA
CBHW060450060326
40689CB00020B/4481